STECK-VAUGHN

Start

Connecting L

MW01711889

Writing Strategies

Consultants

Jim Ford
Training Specialist
Center for Literacy Studies
University of Tennessee
Knoxville, Tennessee

Daniele D. Flannery, Ph.D.
Associate Professor of Adult Education
Coordinator: Adult Education D.Ed. Program
The Pennsylvania State University
Capital Campus—Harrisburg

Barbara Tondre-El Zorkani
Educational Consultant
Adult and Workforce Education
Austin, Texas

STECK-VAUGHN
A Harcourt Company

www.steck-vaughn.com

Acknowledgments

Staff Credits

Executive Editor: Ellen Northcutt
Supervising Editor: Julie Higgins
Associate Editor: Sharon Sargent
Director of Design: Scott Huber
Associate Director of Design: Joyce Spicer
Designer: Jim Cauthron
Production Manager: Mychael Ferris
Production Coordinator: Paula Schumann
Image Services Coordinator: Ted Krause
Senior Technical Advisor: Alan Klemp
Electronic Production Specialist: David Hanshaw

Cover Illustration

Joan Cunningham

Photo Credits

P. 34 Paul Simcock/Brand X Pictures/PictureQuest

Additional photography by Getty Images Royalty Free and Steck-Vaughn Collection.

ISBN 0-7398-6018-6

Printed in the United States of America

1 2 3 4 5 6 7 8 9 0 MZ 08 07 06 05 04 03 02

Contents

To the Learner

Everybody can write, but writing *well* takes some work. Steck-Vaughn's *Start Smart Writing Strategies* will give you strategies to help you improve your writing. By writing better, you will communicate better and get the results you want at school, at work, and in life.

Writing is an active process. Good writers do more than just put words down on paper. They focus on their purpose and how they can best interest readers. They make sure their writing is clear, logical, and appealing. The strategies in this book will help you do the same. You'll learn to plan, write a solid first draft, and polish your writing through revision and proofreading. Try all of the strategies and see which ones work best for you. Your favorites will help you again and again.

As you work through this book, be sure to:

- Fill out the **Identify Your Writing Habits** chart on page 5. This will give you an idea of what your current writing habits are.
- Write down your goals in the **Set Your Writing Goals** web on page 7. Setting goals and checking your progress help you to stay motivated.
- Check out the **Tips** throughout the book. They provide a slightly different approach to the strategies.
- Complete the **Think About It** activities. These help you think about what you have learned. You'll also see the connection to everyday life.
- Create a **Journal.** This book is divided into four main topics. At the end of each topic, you will have the opportunity to write in your journal. Writing thoughts in your own words will help you remember what you've learned and help you track your progress.
- Review what you have learned by completing **What Works for You?** on page 46.

Identify Your Writing Habits

This chart can help you learn about your current writing habits. As you use the strategies in this book, you may notice that your habits are changing.

For each statement, circle A (always), S (sometimes), or N (never).

Before I write, I . . .	always	sometimes	never
think about my purpose and audience (my readers).	A	S	N
choose a topic that works for my purpose and appeals to my audience.	A	S	N
make a plan by getting ideas and organizing information before I start to write.	A	S	N
When I write, I . . .	**always**	**sometimes**	**never**
write an introduction that will get my readers' attention.	A	S	N
write strong paragraphs that are clear, interesting, and grammatically correct.	A	S	N
write a conclusion that ties together the main ideas and leaves a lasting impression.	A	S	N
After I write, I . . .	**always**	**sometimes**	**never**
spend time reviewing my first draft to see if everything is complete.	A	S	N
ask a friend or relative to review my writing and give me honest feedback.	A	S	N
revise my writing by adding, cutting, or reordering information.	A	S	N
proofread my final draft.	A	S	N
check to see that I have everything I need before I turn in my writing.	A	S	N

Set Your Writing Goals

True ease in writing comes
from art, not chance,
As those move easiest who
have learn'd to dance.

Alexander Pope, English poet, essayist, and satirist (1688–1744)

As Alexander Pope noted, writing "with ease" isn't something that comes about by chance. Becoming a better writer comes with practice. Just like dancing, the more you practice and work at it, the easier it is.

Why do you want to become a better writer? Do you need to apply for a job? Do you have reports to write for school? Maybe you want to learn to express yourself better in letters or whatever else you write. Explain in your own words.

....

....

....

....

....

....

....

Consider how improving your writing skills could help you in these areas of your life:

- **Family:** How could improving your writing skills help make your family life better?
- **Work:** How could it help you find a better job or get a promotion?
- **Community:** How could it help you serve your community?
- **Self:** How could it help your education, the quality of your free time, or expand a new interest?

Write your goals for writing in the spaces below. Think about how becoming a better writer will affect your family, your work, your community, and yourself.

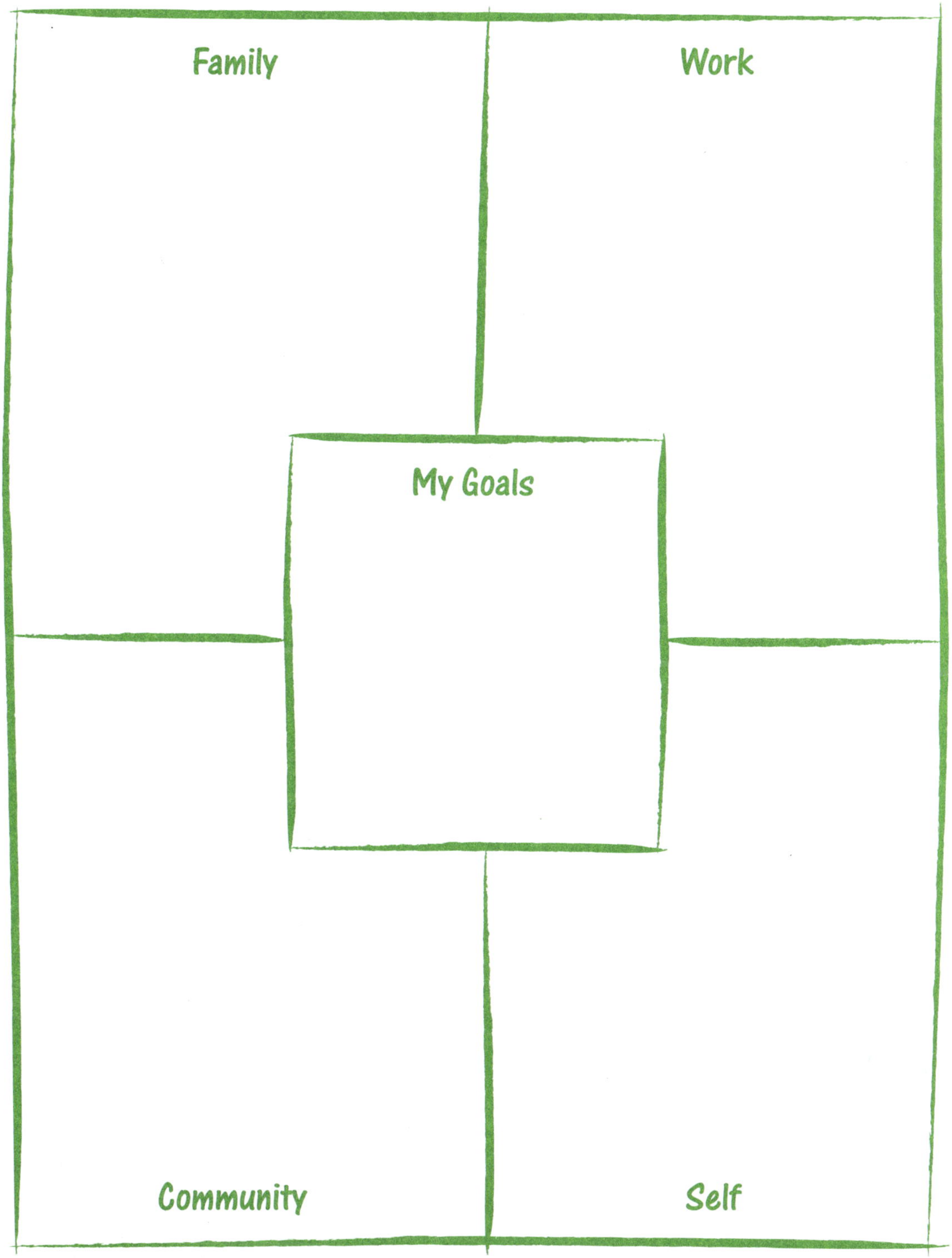

Keep your goals in mind as you work through this book.

Topic 1: Plan Before Writing

In this section, you will learn how to:

- ***identify your purpose and audience***
- ***generate ideas***
- ***organize information***

Before you put pen to paper—or finger to computer keyboard—you need to plan your writing. Just like people plan ahead for vacations, you can plan ahead for your writing. If you just jumped in the car to see where the road takes you, you could waste a lot of time and miss key things.

The same goes for writing. Before you launch into writing, take some time to decide where you want to go, or what your writing purpose is. Determine who will be reading your work. Write your ideas ahead of time and organize them. This will give you a road map to successful writing.

To keep track of your writing ideas, you may wish to jot notes in a separate notebook. Many people write down ideas to remember them. Reporters make notes about possible sources and leads. Busy men and women jot down ideas for their jobs, home projects, and plans with friends or family. You can use your notebook to write notes related to writing.

Strategy 1: Identify Your Purpose and Audience

When you write, you need to know why you are writing. This is your purpose. Next, you need to know who will be reading your work and what will appeal to them. This is your audience.

TIP
Writing requires practice. Set aside a little time each day to write something.

In some ways, planning your writing is like planning a party. You decide the purpose of the party and who will come. Then you plan a get-together where everybody will have a good time.

While writing can have many purposes, some of the most common are outlined in the chart below.

Purpose	Kind of Writing
inform or explain	research paper, book report, business letter, newsletter article, business memo
persuade	letter to the editor or community official, persuasive speech, fundraising or volunteer material
creativity	fiction, such as a short story, poetry
self-expression	letters to friends, emails, journals, personal essays

Once you know your purpose, think about your audience. Who will read your writing? What are their needs? What do you want to communicate to them? How will you make your writing interesting for them?

Sometimes your audience is very clear, such as for a research paper. Of course your teacher will read it and you will have to follow the writing assignment he or she gave you.

Other times, you might need to consider your audience's needs more carefully. Imagine you were asked to write a letter for a community group to get volunteers for a project. Before you write, you might ask yourself: What would interest people in this project? How much do they know already about the project? If *I* were getting this letter, what would persuade me to volunteer?

Atasha attends an English class at a community college. Her instructor asked the students to write an essay on a topic that would help other students do well in the class. First Atasha defined her purpose and audience:

Purpose: To explain

Audience: Students in my English class

Atasha thought about what her classmates would find useful. She also thought about what she, as a student, would like to know. Then she made this list of possible topics:

- *finding your way around campus*
- *getting better study habits*
- *learning how to use the library better*
- *finding places to study on campus*

For her audience of English students, Atasha selected "learning how to use the library better."

Write down the purpose and audience for your writing. Also jot down details such as the due date for a report or the deadline for an article. Keep this notebook with you to record ideas as you write.

TIP
Try to visualize your audience reading your work. How will your writing interest them?

Work with a Partner

Find a newspaper article or advertisement. Read the first two paragraphs and then write down the purpose and audience. Exchange samples with a partner and repeat the activity. When you finish, compare your results. Did you both identify the same purpose and audience? Talk about any differences.

My Sample

Purpose: ....

Audience: ....

My Partner's Sample

Purpose: ....

Audience: ....

Think About It

Think about a letter or some correspondence you received recently. How did it meet your needs as an audience?

....

....

Strategy 2: Generate Ideas

Once you know your purpose and audience, you can tackle your topic. Think of ideas related to the topic before you write.

Ask Questions and Brainstorm

It's important to choose a topic that is not too general or too limited so you can generate a usable number of ideas. If the topic is too broad, like "hobbies," then you might come up with more ideas than you could possibly use. If the topic is too narrow, such as "wood-refinishing tools," then you might not be able to generate enough ideas. A topic like "refinishing old furniture" would give you a reasonable number of ideas to work with.

Ask Questions

A great starting point in generating ideas is to ask basic questions. Take your topic and ask *Who? What? When? Where? Why?* and *How?* Successful writers answer some, if not all, of these questions.

If you know the answers to these questions, write them down first. If you don't know, you'll need to look them up or ask people to help you find the answers. The library or Internet can be very useful. Sometimes it helps to give yourself a deadline for finding the answers. That way you won't let time slip away from you.

Lisette wanted to write a story on her company's history for the company newsletter. Before writing, she answered these basic questions.

Questions	Answers
Who started the company?	Belinda Treman and her daughter Wendy started Belinda's Breads, Inc.
What was the effect on the community?	At first, 10 people were hired, but now more than 200 people have jobs at the company.
When was the company started?	1998
Why did the owner go into business?	Friends loved Belinda's breads. Then small restaurants bought from her, starting the idea she could go commercial.
How did she get funded?	Belinda and Wendy started with investments from friends and family plus a small business loan.

These answers gave Lisette a lot of good information about her company. She wrote the facts in her notebook. She knew she would use this information when she was ready to organize and write the article.

Work with a Partner

Imagine that you have to write a letter of application for a job. Using *Who? What? When? Where? Why?* and *How?*, think of three questions that would show why you are a good candidate. For example, you might ask "Who have I worked for before?" if that shows you worked for a company in the same field.

Questions	Answers
1.	....
....	....
....	....
2.	....
....	....
....	....

3. ....

....

....

Exchange questions and answers with your partner. Discuss how you could use the answers in the letter.

Jot down any key questions related to your topic. Be sure to put a big question mark in front of any questions you do not know the answers to. Fill in the missing answers as soon as you can.

Brainstorm

Brainstorming is a way of collecting ideas by writing whatever comes to mind about a topic. Collecting ideas at this stage is like collecting seashells. As you walk the beach, you pick up as many interesting ones as you can hold. After looking them over, you decide which ones you want to keep.

To brainstorm, plan some quiet time without distractions. Write down any ideas that come to mind about your topic. If possible, brainstorm with a partner or small group to get different ideas.

Write down every idea. Some may be useful. Others may not. This isn't the time to question or criticize. Chances are, you will probably have some very good ideas to use in your writing.

For example, Silvio's supervisor asked him to write some rules about drinking coffee at work. First, Silvio asked himself some questions.

TIP

Don't know what to write? Try brainstorming by talking into a voice recorder.

Who needs these rules?	*Anyone who drinks coffee.*
Why do we need rules?	*Not everyone is paying for the coffee they drink.*
What are other problems?	*The coffee pot is often dirty.*
	No one makes new coffee when the pot is empty.

Next, Silvio got together with a few coworkers to brainstorm ideas. As they brainstormed, they wrote the following possible coffee rules.

Townsend Associates

- *$2/week for coffee*
- *$3/week for coffee*
- *coffee is on the honor system*
- *coffee money goes by chart; check off when you pay*
- *1st person in the office makes the coffee*
- *no leaving just a drop—if you finish it, you make more*
- *last person to leave cleans the pot*
- *everybody takes turns cleaning the pot*
- *pot cleaning goes by schedule; check off when you do it*

After looking at the list, the group crossed off ideas that the majority didn't like. They made choices about ideas that conflicted, like deciding on $2/week for coffee on the honor system. Once the brainstorming group decided on the rules, Silvio wrote them down and posted them in the break room.

Work with a Group

With a group, brainstorm a list of ideas for the topic "ways to study better." Don't forget to list all ideas in the brainstorming session. After the brainstorming, discuss. Put a star by the ideas most people like. Talk about whether or not you could use any of the ideas.

Brainstorm ideas for your writing project and write all your ideas in your notebook. Circle or star the ones that you think are best for your writing purpose.

Think About It

What is your favorite place to think and come up with ideas?

Strategy 3: Organize Information

Imagine you are listening to the radio. You are listening to the weather report and suddenly it switches to local politics. Five seconds later the news switches to a traffic accident. You are definitely hearing the news, but if it's not presented in an orderly manner, it doesn't make much sense. In the same way, you need to organize the information in your writing so it flows in a logical order.

Map Main Ideas and Details

After you've generated ideas, you need to organize them. What are the most important ideas related to the topic? What details support the main ideas? Supporting details usually include facts, reasons, or examples.

You can use a cluster map to show the connection between the topic, main ideas, and supporting details. In some ways a completed cluster map looks like the solar system. Your topic is the sun. The main ideas are the planets around the sun. The supporting details are the moons around each main-idea planet.

To create a cluster map:

1. Write the topic in the middle of a page. Put a circle around it.
2. Write your main ideas in the space around the topic. Circle the main ideas. Draw a line to connect each main idea to the topic.
3. Write supporting details in the space around each main idea. Circle the details. Draw a line to connect each detail to the main idea it supports.

Parker needed to write an article about his town's 200th anniversary for the community newspaper. Before he wrote the article, he organized his ideas in a cluster map.

With this cluster map, Parker organized his information and gave himself a direction to follow when writing his article.

Work with a Partner

Imagine you were asked to write a short report on the benefits of exercise. Create a cluster map on the topic using the diagram below.

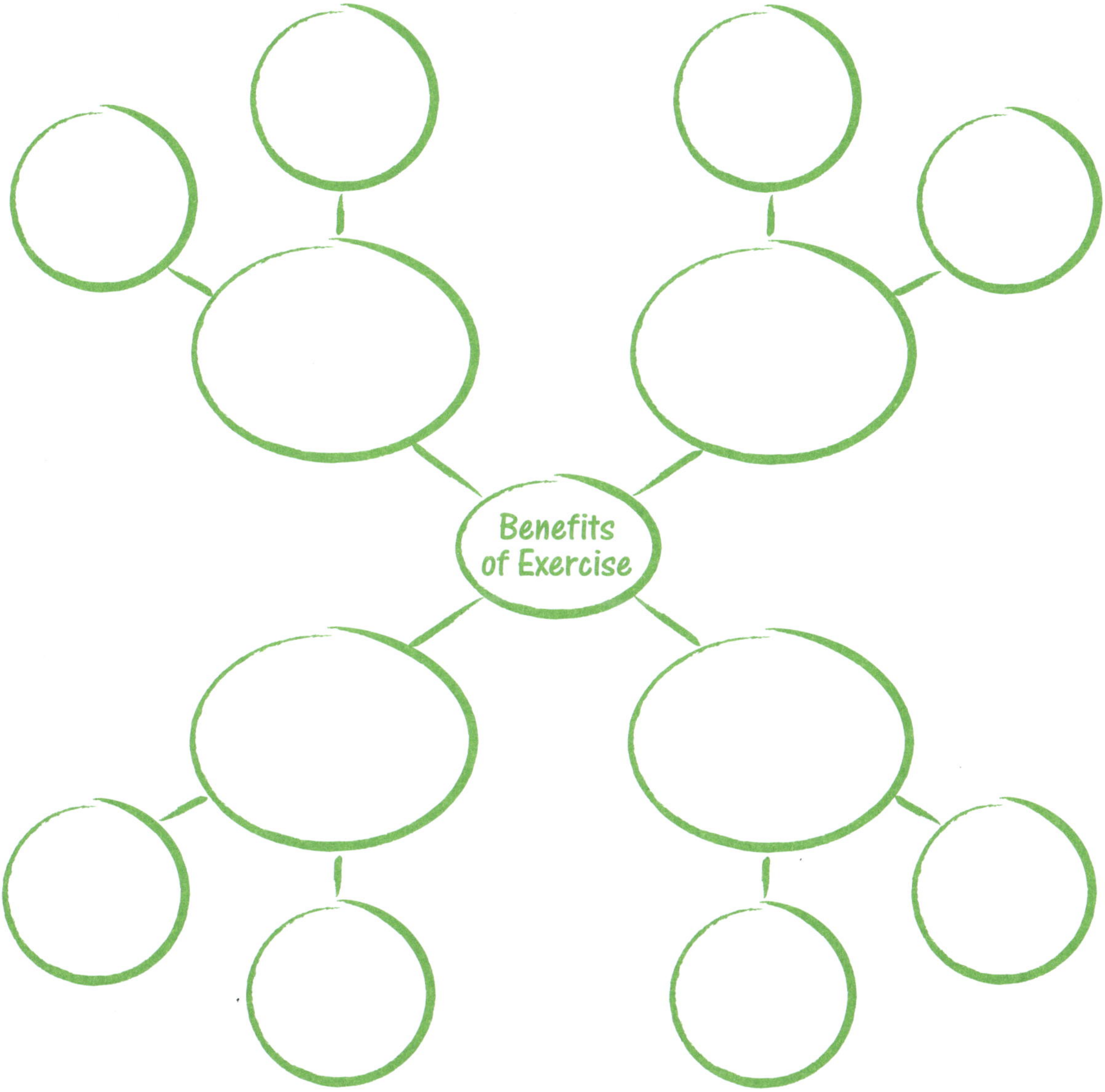

Now exchange cluster maps with your partner. What ideas did you have in common? What ideas were different? Trace each idea back to the topic to see if there is a clear connection. Discuss ways any connections could be strengthened.

Choose a Presentation Style

Once you have a map of ideas and details, you are almost ready to write your first draft. You have only one more step. You need to decide how to present the information you've organized. Each of the following styles presents ideas logically, but in a different way.

Presentation Style	Description	Good For
Time Order	Information is listed in the order in which it occurs.	describing how something took place or evolved over the years; also good for writing about someone's life
Order of Importance	Information is listed from the most important to the least important (or vice versa).	sharing information
Cause and Effect	Information shows how one thing causes another thing to happen.	explaining why something happened or will happen
Compare and Contrast	Information shows how things are alike or different.	persuading readers to agree with your opinion; also good for informing about similarities and differences
Problem and Solution	Information details a problem and how it can be solved.	persuading readers to take action

Ricky, a travel agency employee, found himself answering many questions about a popular island in the Caribbean. He decided to write a short description of the island, comparing and contrasting its two sides.

First Ricky wrote his ideas.

St. Martin/St. Maarten

shared by the French and the Dutch for 350 years
north is French/south is Dutch
friendly relationship

Then he made a compare and contrast chart.

Similarities	Differences
beautiful beaches	St. Martin—French speaking
same weather	St. Maarten—Dutch speaking
nice hotels and restaurants	St. Martin—private beaches designer shops
	St. Maarten—lots of watersports European-style casinos

Finally he organized his information into two paragraphs.

Island Escapades

The Two Sides of the Island of St. Martin/St. Maarten

The beautiful island of St. Martin/St. Maarten has been shared by the French and Dutch for almost 350 years. The French part of the island is in the north and the Dutch part is in the south. A monument at the border describes the friendly relationship between the two countries.

Since the two countries share one island, both St. Martin and St. Maarten have excellent weather and beaches. You can also find fine hotels and restaurants on either side of the island. However, each side of the island still has a unique culture. In St. Martin, the people speak French, but in St. Maarten, they speak Dutch. The French side has private beaches and designer shops, while the Dutch side offers lots of watersports and European-style casinos.

Try It Yourself

Look at the topics below. For each, choose the presentation style that you think would be best. Check your answers on page 47.

1. Write an article on exercise and how it has changed over the past 50 years.

   Article = ... style

2. Write a report on health problems for senior citizens and how exercise could help.

   Report = ... style

3. Write an essay comparing two different sports.

   Essay = ... style

Use your notebook to create a mind map for something you need to write. Then choose the style for presenting the information. Jot that down, too.

Think About It

How hard is it for you to organize information? What could make it easier?

....

....

When You Plan Before Writing

- Identify your purpose and audience. Think about how you can interest your readers.
- Generate ideas. Ask questions and brainstorm.
- Organize your information by mapping main ideas and supporting details and presenting ideas logically.

Journal

Write a few sentences about how you prepared to write in the past. If you didn't really plan, but just plunged into writing, describe that. Now write a new paragraph describing how you will plan for writing in the future. Include specific examples or strategies that you think will be useful.

Next, look at the goals you set on page 7. Note your progress for each of your goals. If you've achieved a goal, put a check next to it and congratulate yourself!

Topic 2: Write Your First Draft

In this section, you will learn how to:

- ***write an introduction***
- ***create strong paragraphs***
- ***write a conclusion***

At last, you are ready to write. All your planning will finally pay off. By looking at your mind map, you know what main ideas and supporting details you want to include. Your presentation style will guide you in ordering the information.

Two very important paragraphs in almost every kind of writing are the introduction and the conclusion. A good introduction and conclusion will help you get your point across.

Strategy 1: Write the Introduction

Your first paragraph should be like a hook on a fishing line. You use it to catch your readers' attention. The introductory paragraph should also present your main idea.

Your introduction can start in many different ways. Each of the following methods will help you interest your audience.

Introductory Method	Example
Ask a Question	How long does the average worker have to work each year to pay off his or her taxes?
Present an Interesting Fact	If you measure from the center of the earth rather than from sea level, Mt. Everest is not the highest mountain in the world.
Take a Stand	We are in danger of losing one of our most precious resources—the rainforest—if we do not act now.
Use a Quotation	"America's healthcare system is sick, and it's up to America's doctors to cure it." —Dr. Martina Whalen
Address the Reader	You probably don't think much about your retirement.

When you're ready to write your introduction, scan through the ideas you've listed in your writing notebook to see if anything strikes a chord. You may recall an interesting detail that initially pointed you to the topic.

Work with a Partner

Choose one of these topics: "getting ready for a job interview" or "healthy eating." Write an introductory sentence for that topic.

....

....

Exchange sentences with your partner and ask: "Is this sentence clear to you?" "Did it get your attention as a reader?" "What suggestions do you have for making it even better?"

TIP

As you write, double space your lines. This gives you room to make corrections later.

Think About It

How do you like to get feedback about your writing? Do you prefer to have the reader write down the suggestions or to talk them over with you?

....

....

Strategy 2: Create Strong Paragraphs

It is important that your writing stands up to a reader's inspection. Strong paragraphs are the foundation of good writing. With strong paragraphs, your readers will understand your point.

Craft Topic and Supporting Sentences

Each paragraph needs to begin with a topic sentence, which tells you what the paragraph is about. The topic sentence is usually the first sentence of the paragraph. Sometimes, however, it can appear in the middle or end of the paragraph. The topic sentence needs to be as interesting as possible. It will catch your readers' attention and encourage them to read on.

The other sentences support the topic sentence. Any sentence that does not shine more light on the topic sentence does not belong in the paragraph. These supporting sentences come from the details in your mind map. They include facts, personal experiences, reasons, and examples.

The supporting sentences are where you can work in your presentation style. Supporting sentences show time order, order of importance, cause and effect, compare and contrast, and problem and solution.

The last sentence of a paragraph is called the closing sentence. Especially in longer paragraphs, the closing sentence brings the details you have developed to an end. Sometimes it sums up the paragraph.

Tabetha wrote the following paragraph for her paper on rap music.

> *Rap music began on the street corner, but it soon entered the musical mainstream. When rap first began, most of the artists dressed in sneakers and sweat suits. It wasn't long before they were wearing expensive clothes and jewelry.*

Tabetha's topic sentence has energy and interest. The next two supporting sentences compare and contrast clothing styles as the music grew more popular.

Try It Yourself

Think of a time in your life when something strange or really funny happened to you. Write a paragraph describing the event. Start with an interesting topic sentence. Then expand this idea with two or three supporting sentences. If possible, share this paragraph with a friend and get her or his feedback.

TIP
If you can't think of a vivid word as you write, use a general term. Later you can replace it.

Use Vivid Language and Active Voice

Everybody notices someone wearing a colorful outfit. Bright or bold colors are interesting. They make us pay attention. Vivid, colorful language serves the same purpose.

Vivid language always helps paint a better picture. For example, the word *color* is a general word. A more specific word is *red*, and a very vivid word is *scarlet*. You can choose words that appeal to the senses, such as *an enormous, rough hand*. Or you can make a comparison so the reader knows what something was like, such as *The snow was a soft, white blanket*.

When you come across a vivid word that you really like, write it in your notebook. Then you can glance through your notebook for the right word when you need to perk up your writing.

Vivid language and an active voice describe things better. Readers can "see" what is going on.

Active voice means writing so the subject takes action. Active voice has energy. The opposite is passive voice, where something is done to the subject. *The cat scratched Alice* is active. *Alice was scratched by the cat* is passive.

Hunt through your writing and catch any passive sentences. Usually a minor change can turn them into active sentences. Also replace any dull nouns, verbs, adjectives, and adverbs with more vivid words and descriptive language.

While you want your writing to be colorful, be careful not to overdo it. Some vivid language is like a peppery spice. A little makes the stew tasty, but too much makes it inedible.

Terris, who had a serious problem with an appliance, wrote the following letter of complaint. First he simply wrote what came to mind. He knew he would go back later and make the paragraphs stronger.

The blender was used without a problem for a week. The third time I used it, however, there was a problem. I was trying to mix mushroom soup so it would be smooth. When I turned the machine on, a loud noise was made, like from the motor. A bad smell came from it. Then the whole machine exploded! There was soup everywhere. I could have been burned.

Then Terris rewrote the letter using active voice and vivid language:

I used the blender twice without a problem. The third time I used it, however, was a disaster. I poured very hot mushroom soup into the blender so that I could puree it. But when I turned the blender on, the motor made a high-pitched screeching noise. A harsh burning smell filled the kitchen. Then the whole machine exploded! Soup sprayed everywhere. I was lucky I was not seriously burned.

The rewritten letter is not only more vivid, but also describes more precisely what happened.

TIP
Try using a thesaurus to find vivid words.

Work with a Partner

Bring in a magazine article that you like. Exchange it with your partner. Read the first two or three paragraphs, paying attention to the words that make it interesting. Circle all of the vivid language and active-voice sentences. Show each other your marked-up articles. Discuss how the circled items help make the article lively. If those words were dull or the sentences passive, would you still want to read it?

Check Mechanics and Grammar

The mechanics of a sentence are the nitty-gritty rules. In some ways, the mechanics are the glue that holds sentences together. Correct grammar makes sentences sound right. Grammar includes pronouns that agree with nouns and subjects that agree with verbs. Agreement means they match up, like *the boy has his book* instead of *the boy has her book.*

When the mechanics and grammar are in place, the sentences look right. They are smooth and understandable.

To improve your writing, here are some rules to follow.

- Begin each sentence with a capital letter.
- End each sentence with a period, question mark, or exclamation point.
- Use complete sentences, each with a subject and verb.
- Make sure each sentence expresses a single idea or detail.
- Avoid run-on sentences. Very long sentences are confusing. Divide them into two sentences.
- Avoid choppy sentences. Combine two sentences into one sentence. Bridge or transition thoughts with words like *because, however,* or *since.*
- Check your spelling. Use a dictionary. Don't rely entirely on a computer spell checker. Most do not know when a word is spelled right but used incorrectly.

Using correct grammar makes your writing easier to understand. Use this checklist to help you.

✔ Subject-Verb Agreement

Your subject and verb must agree in number. If your subject is singular, the verb must be singular. If your subject is plural, the verb must be plural.

Incorrect:	The sales starts on Friday.
Correct:	The sales start on Friday *or* The sale starts on Friday.

✔ Double Negatives

Don't use two negatives in one sentence. The contraction *n't* stands for *not.*

Incorrect:	The store didn't have no more winter coats.
Correct:	The store didn't have any more winter coats.

✔ Pronoun-Antecedent Agreement

Be sure that each pronoun agrees with the noun it refers to.

Incorrect: William and Peter went shopping because he needed a new coat.

Correct: William and Peter went shopping because they needed new coats.

✔ Troublesome Words

Its and *it's.* The apostrophe means *it is. Its* is possessive.

Incorrect: Its my coat.

Correct: It's my coat. (It is my coat.)

Good and *well: Good* is an adjective, so it describes a noun. *Well* is an adverb, so it describes a verb. The only exceptions are verbs of sensation, as in *I feel good* or *The soup smells good.*

Incorrect: We did good on the test.

Correct: We did well on the test.

Fewer and *less: Fewer* goes with nouns you can count. *Less* goes with nouns you cannot count.

Incorrect: There were less people at the store than we expected.

Correct: There were fewer people at the store than we expected.

Lay and *lie: Lay* means *to put. Lie* means *to recline, to rest.*

Incorrect: Lie those items on the counter.

Correct: Lay those items on the counter.

Real and *really: Real* means *true* or *genuine. Really* means *actually* or *truly.*

Incorrect: We were real glad we went shopping.

Correct: We were really glad we went shopping.

Try It Yourself

Correct the sentences below by crossing out words and writing in correct words. Some sentences have errors and others could just be improved. Check your answers on page 47.

1. Since nonsmokers is the majority, they must push for laws that protect their rights.
2. Sam and Alice are going on there honeymoon.
3. The hikers saw black clouds covering the sun and then it started to rain so they ran for cover.
4. She work hard at her new job.
5. The dog lost it's bone.
6. The ballpark was noisy. The ballpark was crowded. The ballpark was hot.
7. I have less quarters than you.

Think About It

What keeps you reading a good magazine or newspaper article?

....

....

TIP

Try the "fire and ice" method of writing. Write while you are "on fire." Then apply "ice" by adding vivid language, rewriting in active voice, checking grammar, etc.

Strategy 3: Write the Conclusion

The last paragraph you write is your concluding paragraph. This paragraph should tie together all your ideas. A strong conclusion will help your readers think about what you have written.

It is important to make the conclusion clear as the "end note" to the writing. Sometimes the paragraph's topic sentence signals the end by including words such as *to conclude, finally,* or *as a result.*

You can end your concluding paragraph in many different ways. The following methods work well for most writing.

Concluding Method	Example
Summarize and Offer a Final Thought	When computers take over jobs, workers must be retrained. These workers deserve a second chance.
Give a Recommendation	Finally, we must take action now to save the rainforest. Write a letter to your city officials, representatives and senators, and presidents of companies harming the rainforest.
Make a Prediction	Once you learn how to use the library, you will wonder how you ever lived without it.
Use a Question	In conclusion, I ask, how many more people will die before lawmakers ban handguns and automatic weapons?

Work with a Partner

Choose a concluding method from the chart above. Use the method to write the final sentence for an article on the joys of going to the movies.

Exchange sentences with your partner. First talk about the methods you used and discuss why you picked the method you did. Then talk about whether the sentence left you with a lasting impression.

TIP

Try reading your writing aloud. You can hear whether your ideas flow smoothly.

Think About It

What was the last article you read that left a lasting impression?

When You Write Your First Draft

- Write an interesting introductory paragraph. Present the main idea and attract the reader's attention.
- Create strong paragraphs. Craft topic and supporting sentences in each paragraph. Use vivid language and active voice. Check grammar and sentence mechanics.
- Write a concluding paragraph that leaves an impression. Tie together the ideas in your writing.

Journal

In a paragraph, describe three new things you will try the next time you write a first draft. Be as specific as possible. Explain why these strategies are worth trying.

Next, look at the goals you set on page 7. Note your progress for each of your goals. If you've achieved a goal, put a check next to it and congratulate yourself!

Topic 3: Review and Revise Your Draft

In this section, you will learn how to:

- ***evaluate your writing***
- ***review details and style***
- ***make changes***

After you've written your first draft, you'll probably feel relieved. There is still more to do, however. Now it's time to go over the draft to see what works and what doesn't work. Then you can work on what needs improvement.

Your first draft is like a colorful rock you find during a walk. It looks pretty good. But when you take the rock home and clean it up, maybe even polish it, then it really looks great. By reviewing and revising your draft, you are polishing it so it shines.

Strategy 1: Evaluate Your Writing

When you evaluate your first draft, it's almost as if you're examining it under a microscope. You are checking it in detail and making sure that it is complete.

You can review your first draft by yourself or ask a friend or relative to be a "peer reader." A peer reader brings "fresh eyes" to your writing, which is especially helpful for lengthy or important writing projects. When you have been thinking about the topic for a while, you may not view the writing as clearly as someone else. Here are some suggestions for evaluating your writing.

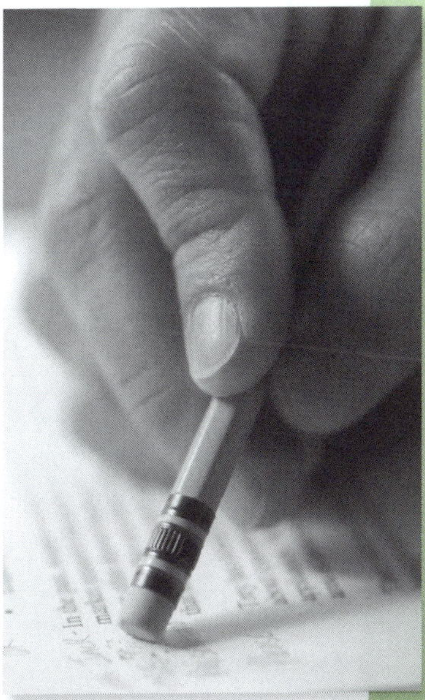

- If possible, evaluate your first draft by yourself and make notes or changes. Then ask a peer reader to evaluate it.
- Try to let your writing "rest" for a day or two before evaluating it. This will give you a little distance from it.
- Don't wait until the last minute. Reviewing and revising takes time.

Evaluate on Your Own

When you evaluate your own writing, you should first look back at your mind map. See if all the main points and supporting details are included in your writing. Be sure that you didn't accidentally leave out something important.

Check through other notes in your writing notebook as well. Was there anything else that you wanted to include?

If you find something you want to add, make a note in the margin of your first draft for now. At the end of your revision process, you can make all your corrections at one time.

Carefully re-read your first draft, asking yourself:

- Does this writing serve my purpose?
- Does this writing meet my audience's needs?
- Does this introduction catch the reader's interest?
- Is the main point clear?
- Do the details help flesh out the main point?
- Do I have the right number of details and are they descriptive?
- Is the information presented in a logical way?
- Does my conclusion tie everything together?

Adam evaluated this paragraph he wrote for an essay. He made changes to improve his work.

Make first sentence clearer.

Give more details.

Needs a conclusion.

My ^hockey team gets together every Saturday morning before practice. ~~Sometimes I watch T.V. before I go.~~ We all meet ^at 8 a.m. at a local coffee shop. ~~Some of us~~ ^Gino, Bo, and Paul eat a big breakfast. The rest of us eat donuts and drink coffee. We like to talk about sports, especially professional hockey. ^This weekly breakfast is a great time for us to socialize before we head off to the rink.

Adam's evaluation showed him where he could improve his paragraph. More descriptive details help the reader "see" the picture. He deleted a sentence that didn't support the main idea. He also added a concluding sentence that made the paragraph stronger.

Work with a Partner

Bring in a non-math textbook. With your partner, pick a chapter at random. Read the first paragraph and see if it gets your attention. Then read the next two paragraphs. Write any ideas you have for improving these paragraphs. What would make them more appealing to you?

....

....

....

....

Discuss whether anything could be done to these paragraphs to help you "see" what is happening better.

Evaluate with a Peer Reader

Successful writers almost always have someone else read what they have written. This is a good way to "test" your writing on an audience. Ask a friend or relative to read your work and give you honest feedback. That includes giving positive comments as well as suggestions for improving the writing.

Before a peer reader reads your work, tell him or her what your purpose is and who the audience will be. Then ask the peer reader to keep these questions in mind while reading:

- Do you understand the main point?
- Does the writing flow logically?
- Do you think anything is unnecessary and should be cut?
- Do you see any "holes" where something should be added?
- Is it interesting to you?

TIP

If you have more than one peer reader, have each person use a different color pen. That way you'll know who made the suggestion.

Jot down any specific questions about your writing for your peer reader. That way you won't forget to go over them. These could include whether how-to steps seem logical, if your argument is persuasive enough, or whether a description brings a certain image to mind.

If you like, ask your peer reader to do certain things while they are reading, such as:

- circle any sentences that seem awkward, choppy, or too long
- circle anything that seems grammatically incorrect
- make notes or comments in the margin or on a separate sheet of paper

When your peer reader is ready to give you comments, ask him or her to start by telling you what was positive or appealing. Then ask for suggestions for improving the writing.

TIP
Try not to be defensive. Give yourself time to let the suggestions sink in.

In your notebook, you might like to list two or three alternative peer readers. Sometimes people are busy and can't help out when you need them.

Soyang asked a peer reader to review her article on her new business. The purpose was to inform. The audience was potential small business owners.

Soyang knew she was not a very strong writer. Therefore, she asked the peer reader to give her very detailed feedback. The beginning of her article looked like this when the peer reader was done.

I absolutely love to cook! Before starting my own business, I would throw huge dinner parties as often as I could. I baked cakes for any occasion. I'd make appetizers for a friend's party and desserts for another dinner the same night. More and more people asked me to make special dishes. I hated my job. I got along well with my boss, but I wasn't happy. Finally, I quit my job. I told everyone I knew that I was now a caterer!—no more free food!

Your enthusiasm makes me want to read more.

This is a really interesting detail.

Maybe this could be softer and smoother.

This detail isn't needed.

To my surprise, the business took off immediately. All I needed was a small-business loan to really get started. Getting a used van to carry the food, supplies, business cards, and price sheets. I had more business than I could handle the first few months. Getting a license was not difficult.

This is not a complete sentence. The details are good, though.

Maybe this sentence should start a new paragraph.

The peer reader pointed out strengths as well as weaknesses. The comments were very specific. These suggestions will definitely help Soyang improve the article.

Work with a Group

On a piece of paper, write a few paragraphs about a job you've had. It could be your current job or one from the past. Do not put your name on the paper. Put all completed papers from the group into a pile or a big bag. Each person should choose a paper that they did not write and act as the peer reader for that paper. Without writing your name on the paper, write your comments in the margins. Give a combination of positive comments and suggestions for improvement.

TIP

When you are a peer reader, give "constructive criticism." Be tactful in offering suggestions for improvement.

Offer to be a peer reader for one of your classmates. Then ask that person to be a peer reader for you.

After everyone is done evaluating, line up the papers face down in a row. Each person can flip up the corner to recognize his or her writing. Review the peer evaluation in private.

Think About It

What kinds of suggestions did your peer reviewer give you? How can you use these suggestions?

....

....

Strategy 2: Review Details and Style

You have already evaluated your writing overall. Now it's time to home in on a few specific areas. In a way, this is like practicing a sport. You play pretty well in a game, but you have a few specific skills that you want to take up a notch.

By strengthening details and smoothing out your presentation style, you will improve your writing. You can usually do this by adding, cutting, or reordering information.

Add Information

If your writing seems incomplete, you can add to it. This chart explains what to add for different problems.

Problem	Add	Method
Cannot "see" what is happening or what something is about	Specific details that help readers visualize and understand	Use descriptive words and phrases, comparisons, examples, or reasons
Choppy movement from one idea to the next	Transition or bridging words and phrases	Use words like *before, since, because, as, therefore, similarly, in addition, but, however*
Does not hold the reader's attention, dull	Vivid words, active voice	Use descriptive words or sentences that have the subject take action

Isabela wrote a description of a childhood fire. After reviewing her writing with a friend, she added information to make it more complete and interesting.

The fire started while we were still asleep. We were
as loud as a passing train,
awakened by the sound of the fire, and a strong smell of
smoke. My brother was the first to figure out what was wrong.
his voice shaking with fear
"It's fire!" he cried, "The house is on fire!" We all stumbled
dizzy with exhaustion and smoke.
outside into the winter night, Our bare feet grew numb
frosty
in the grass. We watched the house burn. It seemed unreal.

Work with a Partner

Make three changes to this paragraph to improve it. Add details, transitional words, or active voice.

An announcement was made by the conductor. "We will have to walk through the subway tunnel to the next station. Everyone follow me!" The passengers walked out through the front car of the train. The tunnel was long and dark. The passengers joined hands and began to walk down the tunnel.

Exchange paragraphs with your partner and discuss the changes you made. How did the additions make the paragraph clearer? Did they make it flow better? Is it now more interesting? Talk about any other ideas you have for improving this paragraph. See page 47 for one example of a revision.

Cut Information

Sometimes when you really get going, you may write more than you need. Your draft may contain too much information. In this case, you need to cut words, phrases, or sentences to improve the writing.

Cutting words or phrases can make your sentences stronger and more effective. Revise any of your writing that falls into these categories.

- **Repetitive.** Repeated words, phrases, or ideas just overstate the point.
  The path was steep and went sharply uphill.
  Revised: *The path went sharply uphill.*

- **Irrelevant.** Irrelevant words or phrases don't contribute to the main idea.
  Petunias, lantana, geraniums, and a ceramic birdbath are lovely in a garden.
  Revised: *Petunias, lantana, and geraniums are lovely in a garden.*

- **Padding.** Padding is extra, unnecessary words or phrases that bulk up a sentence but don't add anything to it.
  Because of the fact that Joanne was promoted, she got a raise.
  Revised: *Because Joanne was promoted, she got a raise.*

Cutting sentences can make your paragraphs more effective. Cut long run-on sentences or divide them into two sentences. Also cut irrelevant sentences that don't tie directly back to the main point of the paragraph.

Kato strengthened this job application letter with the following cuts.

repetitive

irrelevant

padding

My experience makes me very well suited ~~and well qualified~~ for the job of sales representative. I sold makeup door-to-door from 1997 to 1999. I then spent a year as a sales representative for Winstead Publishers. ~~I am very good at talking to people.~~ ~~What I want to say is that~~ I enjoy working in sales and feel that I am very good at it.

Try It Yourself

Revise this paragraph by cutting out repetitive, irrelevant, or padded words. Compare your revision to the answer on page 47.

Eat plenty of low-fat foods and foods that don't have much fat listed on the label. Fish is low in fat and provides protein for the diet. Beans, kidney beans, pinto beans, navy beans, and black beans are completely free of fat and cholesterol and are also an excellent source of protein. Some authorities also consider them the cheapest source. Many believe, at least most scientists that is, that they provide high levels of iron, B vitamins, and vitamin A. Fresh fruit and vegetables are other low-fat foods.

Check for Completeness

Sometimes you may find that your draft is not as clearly organized as it should be. Your ideas may not be in a logical order. To check whether your ideas flow in a way that makes sense, ask yourself these questions.

If your style is . . .	Ask yourself . . .
Time Order	Are my events or steps in the correct time order?
Order of Importance	Do my ideas move from least important to most important?
Cause and Effect	Have I described a specific cause and a specific effect?
Compare and Contrast	Have I clearly shown how things are similar and different?
Problem and Solution	Did I fully explain the problem before I gave a solution?

If you answer "no" to any of the questions, you need to reorder or add sentences or paragraphs. Find any information that is out of sequence and move it to a more logical place. Re-read your writing to be sure your organization is clear.

Felisa wrote directions from her office to the office holiday party. After reading through her first draft, she made changes to make the directions clearer.

TIP
Reviewing and revising might be difficult at first, but the more you do it, the easier it will get.

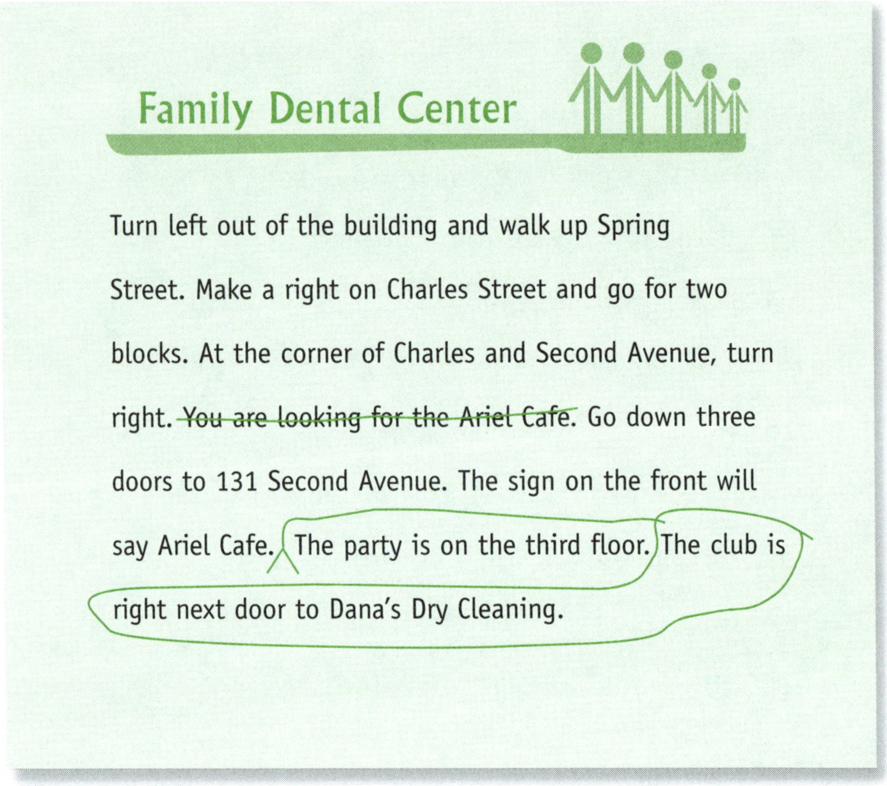
Family Dental Center

Turn left out of the building and walk up Spring Street. Make a right on Charles Street and go for two blocks. At the corner of Charles and Second Avenue, turn right. ~~You are looking for the Ariel Cafe.~~ Go down three doors to 131 Second Avenue. The sign on the front will say Ariel Cafe. The party is on the third floor. The club is right next door to Dana's Dry Cleaning.

Try It Yourself

Write a short paragraph describing one of the following: the steps for making a specific recipe, directions to a park, or the steps for assembling a simple child's toy. Do not write a numbered list of instructions. Write the directions in paragraph form using words such as *first, second, then, next, during, later,* etc.

....

....

....

....

....

....

After you have finished writing, review your paragraph to see if any information needs to be reordered or added. Is this hard or easy for you to do? Think about the connection between logical order and good writing.

....

....

....

....

Think About It

What are your strengths as a writer? What are the areas you could improve?

When You Review and Revise

- Evaluate your writing for completeness. Ask a friend or relative to be a peer reader, especially for lengthy or important writing.
- Review details and style. This includes adding, cutting, or reordering information.

Journal

Write down your impressions of the review-and-revise process. How hard do you think this is? Would it be easier if close friends agreed to be peer readers? In general, do you get wrapped up in the writing and find it difficult to see what changes are needed?

Next, look at the goals you set on page 7. Note your progress for each of your goals. If you've achieved a goal, put a check next to it and congratulate yourself!

Topic 4: Finish Your Final Draft

In this section, you will learn how to:

- ***proofread your writing***
- ***finalize your writing before giving it to your audience***

At last, you are near the finish line—soon your final draft will be ready to stand on its own.

Strategy 1: Finalize Your Writing

There are two more steps before you are completely finished: proofreading and submitting your work.

Proofread

Before your readers see your final draft, you need to proofread. This way you can clean up any last-minute typos and spelling, capitalization, punctuation, or grammatical errors.

Here are some tips to help you proofread.

- **Allow yourself some time between writing and proofreading.** Even a five-minute break helps. The goal is to be able to look at your writing with a fresh perspective.
- **Slow down as you read.** If you read at a normal speed, you won't have time to spot errors.
- **Read aloud.** Reading a paper aloud encourages you to pay attention to every little word.
- **Keep an eagle eye out for stray words.** Something like *a the* might jump out at you. You added *the* but accidentally left in *a*. Now's the time to catch those strays.

After you have marked your draft with any final corrections, rewrite it, retype it, or make the changes using a computer. Compare the new version with your marked-up version to make sure you made every correction.

Try It Yourself

Find a paper, letter, or journal entry you wrote. Go over it again using the proofreading tips. Did you find any mistakes you hadn't noticed before?

If you find you make the same spelling errors over and over, write the correct spelling in your writing notebook. Keep a short list of personal "trouble spots" so you can easily find the right information for spelling, punctuation, or grammar.

Submit Your Work

Once you've made your proofreading changes, you are one step away from victory.

- Check that you have met all the requirements of the assignment. Make a checklist to help you.
- Make a clean copy to turn in.
- Turn in your writing on or before the due date.

Alexis wrote an article on her neighborhood water restrictions for her community newsletter. Before she turned it in, she made a checklist to make sure she had covered all the requirements.

✓ Is it less than 500 words?
✓ Are my grammar and spelling correct?
✓ Does the first sentence catch the audience's attention?
✓ Does the article cover when to water lawns?
✓ Does it talk about how to use less water washing cars?
✓ Does it mention how to take shorter showers?
✓ Does it persuade the reader to use less water?
✓ Does it include a strong conclusion?
✓ Does it include contact information in case the readers have questions?
✓ Is it ready to be turned in before Friday?

TIP
When you're given an assignment, spend time carefully reading the instructions.

Your paper is in! But you are not done yet. Once your paper is returned, review the hints your final audience gives you on how to improve your writing. Recognize the errors you typically make and learn how to fix those errors. Ask your final reader to help you understand the errors you made and what you can do to avoid them in the future.

Work with a Partner

Kent's supervisor asked him to write a memo asking his coworkers to bring in canned goods for holiday baskets. His supervisor said the memo should say exactly what food was needed, who would receive it, the reason it was needed, and when to bring it. The memo should go out in a week with his supervisor's approval. Write out a possible checklist to help Kent make sure he's covered everything before he gives the memo to his supervisor. See page 48 for a sample checklist.

....

....

....

....

....

....

....

....

Compare checklists with your partner. What is the same on both lists? What's different?

....

....

....

....

Think About It

What did you notice about your writing as you reviewed it for the last time?

....

....

When You Finish Your Final Draft

- Proofread. Check your spelling, punctuation, and grammar.
- Submit your work. Use a checklist to be sure you have everything you need before your writing goes to your final audience.

Journal

Write down any ideas that were new to you from this section. Describe one strategy that you will use when putting together your next final draft. Give an example of the way you could use this strategy.

Next, look at the goals you set on page 7. Note your progress for each of your goals. If you've achieved a goal, put a check next to it and congratulate yourself!

What Works for You?

Are your writing habits changing? Review the writing habits you marked on page 5 and answer the questions.

How have my writing habits changed?

What writing habits do I want to work on?

Look at goals you set on page 7. Have you met your goals? Answer the questions.

Which goals have I achieved so far?

Which goals do I want to work on?

Journal

Finish these sentences in your journal.

- These writing skills will help me . . .
- I want to learn to . . .
- I can be a better writer by . . .

Answers

Page 20 Try It Yourself

1. Time Order
2. Problem and Solution
3. Compare and Contrast

Page 28 Try It Yourself

1. Since nonsmokers **are** the majority, they must push for laws that protect their rights.
2. Sam and Alice are going on **their** honeymoon.
3. The hikers saw black clouds covering the sun. Then it started to rain, so they ran for cover.
4. She **works** hard at her new job.
5. The dog lost **its** bone.
6. The ballpark was **noisy, crowded, and hot.**
7. I have **fewer** quarters than you.

Page 37 Work with a Partner

The conductor made an emergency announcement. "We will have to walk through the subway tunnel to the next station. Everyone follow me!" The frightened passengers walked out through the front car of the train. The tunnel loomed ahead, dark and scary. It seemed endless. The passengers joined hands, afraid to be alone in the dark. Slowly, they began to walk down the tunnel.

Page 39 Try It Yourself

Eat plenty of low-fat foods ~~and foods that don't have much fat listed on the label.~~ **[repetitive and irrelevant]** Fish is low in fat and provides protein for the diet. Beans~~, kidney beans, pinto beans, navy beans, black beans~~ **[repetitive]** are completely free of fat and cholesterol and are also an excellent source of protein. ~~Some authorities also consider them the cheapest source.~~ **[irrelevant]** ~~Many believe, at least most scientists that is, that~~ **[padding]** They provide high levels of iron, B vitamins, and vitamin A. Fresh fruit and vegetables are other low-fat foods.

Page 44 Work with a Partner

✓ Does the memo say exactly what food is needed?

✓ Does it tell who will receive the food?

✓ Does it state why the food is needed?

✓ Does it say when to bring the food to work?

✓ Is the memo ready for his supervisor's approval in less than a week?

✓ Are the grammar and spelling correct?